For Now

Also by James Richardson

For Now

James Richardson

COPPER CANYON PRESS
PORT TOWNSEND, WASHINGTON

Cover art: Fermi National Accelerator Laboratory / Science Photo Library

Copper Canyon Press is in residence at Fort Worden State Park in Port Townsend, Washington, under the auspices of Centrum. Centrum is a gathering place for artists and creative thinkers from around the world, students of all ages and backgrounds, and audiences seeking extraordinary cultural enrichment.

LIBRARY OF CONGRESS CATALOGING-IN-PUBLICATION DATA

Names: Richardson, James, 1950– author.
Title: For now / James Richardson.
Description: Port Townsend, Washington : Copper Canyon Press, [2020] |
Identifiers: LCCN 2019056174 | ISBN 9781556595790 (paperback)
Subjects: LCGFT: Poetry.
Classification: LCC PS3568.I3178 F67 2020 | DDC 811/.54—dc23
LC record available at https://lccn.loc.gov/2019056174

98765432 FIRST PRINTING

COPPER CANYON PRESS
Post Office Box 271
Port Townsend, Washington 98368

www.coppercanyonpress.org

Acknowledgments

Poems in this collection first appeared in the following publications:

Academy of American Poets Poem-a-Day	"On the One Hand and on the Other"
The Adroit Journal	"Not a Bird," "Not an Artichoke"
AGNI	"Wanderer's Night Song (II)"
The American Poetry Review	"Epilogue in Stone," "Vectors 5.2—PG-50"
The Common	"I Remember Stopping on a Little Bridge in 1972"
Copper Nickel	"Vectors 5.1—Otherwise"
Frogpond	"*Crows*," "*White butterflies*"
Harvard Review Online	"When yellow leaves, or none, or few do hang..."
Lips	"Parks Department"
Modern Haiku	"*Moon still out*," "*Noon—the sun*," "*Winter sunset*"
Narrative	"Bird," "*Flies at our diner*," "From Up Here," "The Touch"
The Nation	"Grid"
New England Review	"Incredulous Essay on Hummingbirds"
The New Yorker	"For the Children," "Here," "On the Fly"
Plume	"With a Grain of Salt," "Ode to the Paper Clip"
Plume Poetry 7: New Poems 2018	"After the Flood"
Solstice	"Astronomer," "Pines"

Thanks to Michael Wiegers, Joseph Bednarik, and everyone at Copper Canyon for a decade of support; to John Pierce for his aerial view and his microscopy; and to that most excellent poet David Orr for taking a look and for regular beers. And to Connie Hassett for Everything, which happened to include reading this book as many times as I did.

Contents

5 After the Seasons

For Now

1 Overtures

The Touch

for Connie

Forty years on, the wine
we poured out on the lawn
leaving the party together
reaches the ocean.

On the One Hand and on the Other

Consider the palms. They are faces
with their eyes closed, the ten spread fingers
soft exclamations, sadness or surprise.
They have smile lines and sorrow lines, like faces.
Like faces, they can be hard to read.

Somehow my palms, though they have held my life
piece by piece, seem young and pale.
So much has touched them, nothing has remained.
They are innocent, maybe, though they guess
they have a darker side that they cannot grasp.

The backs of my hands, indeed, are so different,
shadowy from the sun, all bones and strain,
that sometimes I think they are not mine.
But time on my hands, blood on my hands—
for such things I have never blamed my hands.

One hand writes. Sometimes it writes a reminder
on the other hand, which knows it will never write,
though it has learned, in secret, how to type.
That is sad, perhaps, but the dominant hand is sadder,
with its fear that it will never, not really, be written on.

They are like an old couple at home. All day,
each knows exactly where the other is.
They must speak, though how is a mystery,
so rarely do they touch, so briefly come together,
now and then to wash, maybe in prayer.

I consider my hands, palms up. *Empty,* I say,
though it is exactly then that they are weighing
not a particular stone or loaf I have chosen
but everything, everything, the whole tall world,
finding it light, finding it light as air.

Incredulous Essay on Hummingbirds

Whir of spokes, little splash
of tachycardia—
everything about them is too vivid

to believe,
as if they were illustrations somehow
lifted from the page,

even their obvious hovering
a kind of concealment, the wings
invisibly swift.

Some weigh less than a penny, little more
than my first thought
when I see one—*this*

can live?

*

Infallibly the surprise
of their first droning in the garden,

all danger
of frost past,

freezes me (the sting
of a bee that loud would kill

instantly).

White blooms are flame enough
to draw them, seeing what they see

of ultraviolet colors,
to us, mere rumors.

The whirling turbine
of the wings, the heart strobing
a thousand times a minute—

Time must rage
in them. If I touched one,

immediately

my hair would silver, and my bones
gray.

Naturally, their *torpor,*
as it's called, is in proportion
steep and dark, a 90 percent
drop in metabolism
that an insomniac could envy
more than flight,

even the tiny light
in their heads
off
that they would need to dream.

*

Busy winds, tiny flywheels loosed
from day's machine—

no way, from the mere
sipping of nectar, could they build

feather and speed and tendon,
yet seeing them snap up

insects when they think
no one's looking
is faintly a letdown. I wanted
sweetness to be that strong.

                    *

It isn't

humming, is it?—
the note changing
more slowly than the weather.

We'd have to listen
all summer, and to all of them at once,

to hear the whole song,
its secrets hidden
right there in the open

from us, always too lightly turning
to our smaller, quicker tasks,

as if anything at all could be an ending.

Vectors 5.1

Otherwise: Aphorisms and Ten-Second Essays

The secret to unhappiness is knowing exactly what you want.

*

They make a point of seeming dissatisfied, as if it were less important to love their lives than to prove they aren't fooled by them.

*

Somewhere in the multiverse, the theory goes, some duplicate of me has everything I could imagine wanting. Should that make me happier or sadder?

*

Though it's not what I ordered, I don't say anything. Maybe it won't be great, but it won't be disappointing in quite the way what I chose could have been.

*

I like having choices a lot better than using them.

*

So often it would have been better to doubt my confidence, but I would have needed more confidence in my doubt.

*

Dreams hurt each other.

*

I'm going to start calling it *predicting the Past,* since so much of what I want to know about the Future is how I'll feel then about what I'm deciding to do Now.

*

What's called creativity is an accident we learn to keep having.

*

Luck whispers *You deserved me.*

*

Silly to worry about the freedom of the will since most of me arrives from beyond its reach: weather, history, accident, you.

*

Self-expression? The things that sound exactly like me are exactly what I try to keep myself from saying. You have to run the water awhile before it's cool and true.

*

I'm blissfully solitary for a minute—and then who shows up but myself?

*

Let's be fair about the limits of language: often enough what it says is actually better than what we were thinking, though maybe not as good as what we thought we were thinking.

*

It's about as easy to find a truth no one has ever said as a mistake no one has ever made.

*

I tripped so badly I danced.

*

How embarrassing to be a god, stripped of all your excuses. Everyone would know that everything you were, everything that happened to you, everything that came out of your mouth was exactly what you had wished.

*

The unbeliever's prayer: *Help me so subtly I don't notice. Be the luck I can take credit for.*

*

Mountains are always moving. It's less a matter of faith than of patience.

*

Maybe I'm not lost, just a little too certain I should be somewhere else.

*

The road not taken also would have gotten me home.

*

It always makes sense to say *You're alive, what else do you want?* But only to yourself.

For the Children

They were unutterably lovely, the aliens,
when finally we knew them, when at last we understood
they had lived and moved among us from the beginning

in bodies the image of ours, though smoother, eyes wider,
as if the world were a little darker for them, or more wondrous,
and we loved them as wildly and deeply and helplessly

as our first loves, our dreams, our lost ones, all at once,
though we knew they were wilder and deeper than we were, and freer,
and loving them only deepened our loneliness.

When they gathered on evening corners, faintly luminous,
and their murmuring rose in urgency, calling on stars,
we feared they would leave us for worlds far, far beyond us,

though we dared not ask, in their language so eerily ours,
Will you carry us with you?—lest they look away, bored
with our dullness, our burdensome love, our ignorant dying.

What could we, after all, with our dim minds, our narrowed sensoria,
know of the lightning of their thoughts, the storm of their joys?—
or their sorrows, for sorrow was theirs, they were lords of sorrow.

Why in the world these creatures, immortal and perfect,
should be so gloomy and aimless was beyond us,
yet they grew so slowly into the unprecedented lives

we had thought they would seize instantly as their right
that it seemed the long, long future brooding over them
was so heavy they could hardly bear it forward one little step.

And at last they dismissed the fantastic travels, faster than light,
that had landed them only here, and their magic technologies
that had taught them, it seemed, what anyone could have told them,

and they ceased to gather on corners, dreaming of rescuers,
and glanced, if at all, only sidelong at the stars.
Maybe some earthly pathogen had worn them,

or the weakness of our yellow sun had left them so wan
that even their radiant children could not tell them from us
when they sat with us, sipping at coffee, a little more patiently now,

enduring our sadness, our sad adoration, even our sad relief
that life was a little less possible than once we had hoped,
since who else in the vast, small universe still knew

that they were as luminous and unutterably lovely
as our first loves, our dreams, our lost ones all at once,
so impossible they were beautiful, so beautiful they were true?

What It's Like

Say the moon is as small as it looks
and I place it on my table,

half lit, half in darkness,
as the moon always is,

with a glow that seems to come from inside,
shadow that seems to come from inside.

I say it is all I could want,
shadow I cannot light,

light I cannot darken with my hand,
and more beautiful than the moon

you think you see, and realer,
one side so hot, one side so cold

I can hardly hold it,
though somehow *freezing and burning*

I can hold it.

Dark night,
the moon has snowed itself
out of the sky.

On your long
gray hair, snow lasts
a little longer.

Snow on my page—
no harm
if it's cold enough.

From Up Here

From the 5th floor, by a window
no one can open, I think I can hear,
when the bus stops just at sunset,
its gasp open and sigh shut,
its struggle away from the curb.

While those it discharges, mostly alone,
a few pausing to talk, set off
north south east west from the corner,
all bending forward, as if into a wind
that blows from every way at once.

2   Now and Here

Now

How long is the Present? Say it's the Planck time,
the 10^{-44} second
in which light spans one grain of space;
or that longer instant anyone needs
to see a flashed word or a single frame
before it blurs into the stream of a film;
or that small eternity, maybe half a second,
of a face clouding, of eyes going vague.

Maybe it's short-term memory,
the two to three seconds of repeating
a four-beat line of poetry,
or *555-0363*
over and over heading to the phone;
or maybe the twenty minutes of *Just a minute;*
or the sleep-wake cycle's ninety,
which is also the length of a lunch, or a mood,
or the longest a meeting can go without more coffee.

Perhaps it's a day, or a year. Or the civil present:
the four years of a presidential term
or a college; the median length, sadly,
of marriages that end in divorce;
the interval of Olympics and leap years.
Or maybe those less definable moments, or ages,
or stanzas before we're ready to say,
you and I, or random anyones,
Now we are really on the same page.

And *when* is the Present? *Now?* But then,
how much of our lives is worry and fantasy
that are neither anywhere nor anywhen.
I'm feeling, right now, that it's off and on,

the Present, that more of it happens
in vistas, or at small tables, or on trains,
alone, or in the very best company.
It's like driving parallel to a very long lake
seen now and then as brightness through dark trees.

Even on good days there are long, long whiles,
by definition lost to memory,
that are nothing in particular,
when suddenly sitting out under the leaves
(I'm tempted to think it has to do with leaves)
and speaking of nothing very weighty,
here we are, or there it is, or there it has been
for all eternity: the Present.
                        Our neighbor,
did his light just now go on,
or is it now just dark enough to see?

Not an Artichoke

My vegetable love should grow
vaster than empires, and more slow

Marvell, "To His Coy Mistress"

Fifty minutes minimum
to steam one, time we could use
to winnow the inbox, mow the lawn,

or sit and talk a little
too long and fall,
again, behind.

Seems we resolve
daily to get one started
first thing, or in 4:30's

Unhappy Hour, but when
we don't, and it ages
in the dank fridge, passed up

again and again for quicker dinners,
let's not blame
poor Time!

Those resolutions,
after all,
are to be less ourselves,

so maybe studying
more deeply what we know already
we can't get enough of—

the blunt zucchini,
the pliant eggplant, the already
ready tomato—really is

the way to go, though older
and fainter grows the memory
of stripping with our teeth

the softness from the undersides
of those leaves, an almost-nothing
tasting, really, like nothing

but artichoke. Even in tiers
of produce it's far-fetched—
more hardware

than comestible—its very name,
so downstream from the Arabic
al-hursufa that it means,

to the ear, something
about *heart* and *choking,* which
I guess you could,

on the sharp leaves. *Milicia,*
Neruda calls it—O little soldier,
newel, cupola,

grenado, thurible,
finial, gauntlet
hivelet, thistle,

how would the darkness
differ if we slipped
off to sleep

with those words only
other people use
on our lips?

NO POSTAGE
NECESSARY
IF MAILED
IN THE
UNITED STATES

 CopperCanyonPress.org

BUSINESS REPLY MAIL

FIRST-CLASS MAIL   PERMIT NO. 43   PORT TOWNSEND WA

POSTAGE WILL BE PAID BY ADDRESSEE

Copper Canyon Press
PO Box 271
Port Townsend, WA 98368-9931

What do you think?

BOOK TITLE: _____

COMMENTS: _____

_____

Our Mission:

Poetry is vital to language and living. Copper Canyon Press publishes extraordinary poetry from around the world to engage the imaginations and intellects of readers.

Thank you for your thoughts!

Can we quote you? ☐ yes ☐ no

☐ Please send me a catalog full of poems and email news on forthcoming titles, readings, and poetry events.

☐ Please send me information on becoming a patron of Copper Canyon Press.

NAME: _____

ADDRESS: _____

CITY: _____ STATE: _____ ZIP: _____

EMAIL: _____

MAIL THIS CARD, SHARE YOUR COMMENTS ON FACEBOOK OR TWITTER, OR EMAIL POETRY@COPPERCANYONPRESS.ORG

Copper Canyon Press
A nonprofit publisher dedicated to poetry

Three thirty, four—
trying to float
   in an inch of water.

The car that lit our room,
lost,
   lights it again.

Three thirty, four—
I turn on my right side
   not to hear my heart.

With a Grain of Salt

Salt on black silk
are the stars,
and legendarily

slick crystals
line the red-dark
entries of the underworld,

and when the spreader grinds by
in a whiteout, you breathe it
down on your tongue

invisibly, and even dissolved
darkly in dark waves
it will burn a wound.

                    *

Deer and other
eaters of leaves
are drawn to salt licks,
whereas carnivores (blood is enough)
don't seek it. As for us,

our bodies hold
a good half pound
of salt, though you are mostly
tasteless to yourself—

unless, say, you bite your lip,
or in some teary, moonlit theater
of balked passion
(alas, I've done this) kiss
your own damp wrist.

*

John Evelyn oddly
called newfangled
New World sugar
Indian salt—and yet

taste-test
a single white
crystal of either on the tip

of your finger. That first
tiny instant—
sting or sweet?

*

No ant, no rot
dares its white plain.
Microbes that touch

its sheer thirst:
dust. Everyone
knows by now the *salary*

we sweat for is, at root,
salt money,
but even joy's grape

contains a trace, never mind
the wine-dark sea, and surely
you taste on a warm

brow or lip
the work or fever
or whatever whatever
we want from each other.

*

Seeing my yearning,
Grandma would say

*Do you know
how to catch a bird?*
(her riddle
older than Evelyn)

Put salt on its tail.

*

Salt on black silk
are the stars.
            There are,
let us not forget,
white fires.

Dawn, our neighbor's lights
pale
　　from staying on all night.

Moon still out—
dew
　on a cold shovel.

Where lightning all night
struck and struck,
　　nothing.

Essay Slightly in Advance of the Discovery of Element 120

It'll
be something like the ninetieth
unique and elementary and irreducible
metal
that no one can tell from any of the others
(maybe you're forgetting
lutetium, ytterbium, et cetera?)

and utterly abstract,
since never will there be sufficient
atoms in one place to see its color,
nor in the vast
galaxy to form a tack,
which would, before the hammer
half-descended
(given its microsecond half-life),
unexist.

Four elements
was enough, right?—
earth and water,
fire and air—though sure
everyone wants
to be different,
everyone wants a name on the door,
everyone wants to feel
no one has ever felt this way before.

But I'm with the alchemists.
There must
be ways to change base metal
into gold or, if you're Midas

and starving, to persuade inedible
gold fruit-shapes once again
to be apples.

Don't tell me
iron isn't bronze
at sunset, or that bronze
is still bronze in an iron dawn.
I'm with
La Rochefoucauld when he avers
We are sometimes as different from ourselves
as we are from others.

I remember the child
who used to be you. She brought a bowl
of her first snow indoors
for its white burn, and after a nap,
and sadly, washed her hands clear
in what could not have been water.

I remember a thousand days—
or to be candid,
I remember them all as one—
when the hundred elements in the room
were all one
to me, because the feeling *Oh, that this day*
would never end

had ended.

Just Now

The Future is infinite, the Past is infinite, but only Now takes time.

The Modern Poem of the Stars

this huge stage presenteth nought but shows
whereon the stars in secret influence comment

Shakespeare, sonnet 15

The sky's a little hazy, only a smattering will be visible
for this, the Modern Poem of the Stars. Yes, there are fewer
than there used to be, and less because of burnout,

early retirement, and supernovas
of unrequited stellarness
than that pollution and skyglow and whatever else

comprises Modern
have made it more difficult, whatever we pretend,
to see beyond ourselves. In Shakespeare's time

the headlong expansion of the universe
had not yet gotten out of hand, or else
our feelings were still large enough to feel its edges,

and anyone walking late on a summer night
could hear the stars *in secret influence comment,*
but now that we are Modern

and Einstein has limited information
to the speed of light, we know stars are too distant
for critical remarks. Even in our tiny galaxy

only a tiny fraction are close enough
so that any hint of us has ever reached them.
Rigel, at 1400 light-years right next door,

has never seen written English; Becrux,
at 460, is about to witness Shakespeare's birth.
If you're fifty years old,

only 133 stars are near enough
to know you exist, a number strikingly similar
to the 150 relationships social scientists say

(Facebook notwithstanding) is the maximum
we can truly attend to. That star, there, is seeing me
faintly in Virginia as I was

forty-some years ago. (I know who it is! Sorry!)
That one is watching me in Boston, just
a few years later. (What was I thinking?)

Even Sirius, alas, the closest star
visible to what we call the naked eye,
and which in this Modern Poem of the Stars

we know is a binary, might be regarding
with a certain stern ambivalence
those hard days, nine years back,

when I let my parents go, and any advice
or secret influence those great lights
might vote to dispense would appear

nine years from now, maybe at expired addresses
and in closed accounts, or while my hemisphere
was turned away—their faint voices

so much like conscience, though odds are they were meant
for someone completely different, in lands
far from this one, and millennia ago.

It's not just stars! I didn't hear my parents
till they were gone, and my own words
arrive too late, or maybe it's too early,

for everyone younger, and theirs for me, and all
the books I read, so brilliant—
they must have said it all, yet here I am,

thinking why didn't anyone tell me how it would be
now? But Einstein says there is no Now
we can all be in. There will be no Heaven, no blaze

of simultaneity and telepathic unity
where all of us know what all of us have been thinking
second by second—the vanity and silliness and lust—

and thank God, since we could never stand it,
since we are Modern, our sins so ours, so *us,*
that not even for forgiveness would we bear

the dissolution of being known,
not even to be delivered from death
would we die of embarrassment. Thus it happens

that we, and our children, and our children's children
need longer than ever to mature
into ever frailer and more multitudinous selves,

many and lonely and fleeing like the stars,
and our years are light-years. Remarkable, isn't it,
that science at last has given us the universe

we wanted all the time? Look up, look out
at the stars! Well, as I mentioned, it's hazy tonight
and only the closest and brightest are in evidence:

Jupiter, Venus, Mars, which are not stars at all
but planets. It's hard to remember,
so cold they look, that it's yourself you're seeing up there

in the middle of the night, or anyway reflected sun
from the day you just left still going on,
or tomorrow getting under way without you.

Trillions of stars—
over 7th Ave.
just four.

Strange bar, no one knows
I'm brilliant,
rich, young.

Here

How every way you look the fog
is thicker than where you are.

3   It Was When

Grid

All energy, to that engineer,
the Soul, is the same.

Today's illumination might have come,
way back, from either love or pain—

no whiff, when the light flicked on,
of coal or falling water or uranium.

Out of the Rain

Those were the oldest rains,
the animal rains,
the no-school, sweet,
and summer rains.

Nothing to do but watch all morning
and all afternoon
Gale Storm, December Bride,
I Married Joan.

Were you six, was I nine?

*

The rain rained rain.
We stretched from bed to bed
our blanket tent,
and lived all day invisibly
in a warren of gray light
(our small TV
was black and white)

with *Topper, The People's Choice, The Millionaire.*

All repeats!

*

Beneath the tent
(as if the rain might rain indoors)
we played Jan Murray's *Treasure Hunt*!

He had thirty chests of treasure.
We set three in a line.

One was a cigar box
smelling of wet autumns,
one was a real treasure chest,
cedar, the size of a hand,
with a brass clasp and a script
Ft. Ticonderoga.

I still have it!

*

I would put in, or you would,
treasures you or I could win:

the stinger of a horseshoe crab,
a hopscotch stone the mind could guide,
the feather of a dove,
a vestige of a dinosaur,
a bullet from the Civil War.
(It had to be
something it would hurt to give.)

Pick one!

*

The tie clip in the shape of a sword,
the big black bolt
from the undercarriage of—
who knows, the night?
The gold-winged moth with azure veins,
a marble white as an eye.

Even a dime
(your whole allowance)
or a quarter (that was mine).

They were real silver then.
They were made of rain.
They could (we might!)
turn into anything.

(I wanted to be? *Mickey Mantle.*
You? *A lion.*)

Open one!

*

Brother, I never opened
why that gun went off.

How could you (did you?)
mean to die?

So many years
since I've said *you* to you.

(Were you nineteen,
was I twenty-two?)

*

The waiter clacks down
a glass of rain.

The body's
60 percent rain.
The ocean, rain.
The whole past,

rain,

and *Richardson,* our name—
I've yearned

to tell you this—an anagram
for *rain chords!*

Pick one!

                *

A famous stamp, a Yankee card,
some sea-glass bluer than sea blue,
a ring, real emerald!

(Did we let each other open
all three chests?
I hope we did. I think we did. We did!)

                *

Those long, long rains,
those silver rains, young rains,
those no-school, summer,
warm and animal rains
way back when rain was sweet—

it is still sweet!

I Remember Stopping on a Little Bridge in 1972

                    It is so late
it is early, and there, once again,
is that thrilling and disturbing bird
of dawn, its four notes,
one two THREE, four climbing
a little way up into the future
and back down, and once again
everything that's mine is in a rental truck
or in the future.

I should tell this boy
who has pulled over by a little river
just so he can breathe, this boy
wishing so hard for this to be over
that he has called me here—I should tell him
to relax, that it's going to be OK,
that he'll get there by sunset,
sit among boxes with a six-pack,
letting the TV run on and on.

I won't tell him about the breakdown, only a day,
I won't tell him about the worse things
that will break in a week, a month, a year,
the ones he would think he could not get over
and still be himself, the ones
he would hate me for getting over.
I tell him, however it is we're speaking,

that it's just fine here in the future,
so that in a few minutes he can go on,
as he did. I think him into the truck,
which hesitates but starts

this time. Now on the waters fast enough to hear,
the reflected moon
lets go, sweeps downriver.

Rain—
what have I left
out in the rain?

Through the rain
raining, can't see
where the rain ends.

It couldn't be
less like tears,
the rain.

On the Fly

Though twice I forgot them
in that apartment between two lives,
when I was—well,
what *was* I doing?—
it is well to consider the flies

and their flights, the soft stumble
of the moth fly,
or the pixel drifting up
from a peach so loose it's torn
by its stone,
or the soot fly, or the evening

      hoverfly,

the sweat fly, the deer fly,
or the laser flight
of the corpse fly, which from miles away

hears your breathing
pause
and soon too soon homes in.

*

Though mostly it is houseflies
we notice,
taking off backwards
(swatters must compensate)
as if they'd suddenly remembered something.

*

Magnets, magnets!
shrilled my landlady,
when I got back from weeks
of doing what I was doing.
She meant, of course
(I had forgotten
to tie my trash),
maggots.

*

Precise in their prissy,
hand-wringing way,

flies are by our lights
filthy, walking in shit,

though light, light on your brow
is their sixfold grip.

*

Some things in a life
happen once, but then again,
some happen twice.

More weeks away,
and I strode into my kitchen—wrong,
dark at noon,

its one window
inwardly black,
flat black with flies.

*

They are necrophiliacs,
sure, but shriven in passing
through the strait, white gate

of a fly's egg, maggots,
though they turn our stomachs, come out
pure as magnets.

So much more pointed than a scalpel's
is their distinction, cell by cell,
of dead from viable flesh

that surgeons defer to their soft mouths
to clean wounds,

so hard and true it is
to leave life carefully behind.

Flies at our dinner—
won't eat much sings the tiny
ghost of my mother.

Astronomer

And I said flat out the stupidest thing *ever,*
and my brain (I'm sure she could hear it)
was a crumpled page uncrumpling in high flames,
and I was slipping sideways
through a glass door into a night so far
and cold and cruel that I felt freedom,
and laughter, though I couldn't say whose,
on that unprecedented evening
when I was the first ever to notice the stars.

Ode to the Paper Clip

O knot in two dimensions,
tiny maze, shine on the rug,
little animal endemic

to desks, self-perpetuating
unendangered species,
trumpet too fine to sing!

You must, since everything
is like everything, also be like me,
though at the moment I can't think how.

I don't have the baker's
floured boards, a pick for anthracite,
a van with racks of pipe, but paper clip,

I have you, essential tool
of the Service Sector, subcategory
Helping Professions, who assist

information everywhere
in its dance like the bee's
shaky rendition

of where the flowers are
for any of its fellows
who might want to follow.

It's harder to say what
we do, in our white
collars (though I

affect blue), every day a different
same thing, or same
different thing. How I

dreaded, when young, the terrible
smallness of the life to come:
baking a single loaf

forever, climbing a ladder
with two nails between my lips
forever, correcting

a single uncorrectable essay
forever forever forever,
the future a darkened mountain

with one pinprick of light
imagination couldn't open
into a single day I could imagine

living minute by minute. Even
these minutes, modest but unalone,
watching my feet go dark light dark

on the subway, one guy
slumped, post-work, both of us
thinking without thinking it,

How does he live?—when out of my pocket
you appear, O paper clip,
dulled with crumbs, humbler even

than the useless penny, change back
from nothing at all! How did I forget
you would be here with me,

minute by minute, in any
basket of miscellany, any drawer—
for a room without minutes

is more likely than a room
without paper clips, ready to join
any two thoughts days souls

into a new thing. Truly we call
poet that part of anyone
that knows it has no job,

or every job. As you do!
Vaulting tower
of a finger-long Verrazano,

hairpin interchange,
impossible pipeline
that ends where it begins or,

who knows, begins where it ends—
touching at once
the first page and the last!

Always I hear—O retired
exclamation point! O social metal!—
that sound you make, all of you,

when my blunt fingers enter
a little dark nest of you
to elicit one, a faintly excited

tinny rain, a chorus
of murmurs *we are only
what we are together!* Oh, to have lain

all night with my love on a bed
of paper clips, such pure connection,
our every motion spoken!

Parks Department

It had no other name, my *paper-stabber*,
an ice pick jammed thick end in a broom handle,
or the job I loved for a summer, *paper-stabber*,
spearing cups and papers from the asphalt
with a sidewise slide so the point didn't blunt,
and slipping them into my bag with a gloved hand.

My task was wandering the small downtown,
leaving my lots unlittered as the dawn.
It was too early to care that no one saw me
in my faded Everything and work boots
even when they saw me. I could still be sure
I wasn't what I wore, I wasn't what I did,
I wasn't even what I was, a college kid,
and anything could happen: I found
bright change in abundance, and once, a ten.

Was it really a whole summer, or just a few hours
one sunrise, or was it my whole life
(which, winter or spring or fall, was a kind of summer)
that it was enough to be taken for granted,
since I was the servant of a great beauty,
regarding all the world with a love
so distant and vague and impartial
no one could be burdened, no one could refuse?

4 Elemental

Not the Ocean?

Landlocked here
in Princeton—haven't seen
the ocean in a year.

Is it still there?

The footage
last night on the news looked...
maybe archival?
And the rumors
are terrible—

no sharks, no whales,
the reefs bleached
to a sterile paleness,
and an eighth continent,
petabits
of polystyrene and acrylic,
replacing the Pacific.

Are you sure?

Those white, anonymous
filets they sell me
in old-style paper
might be from farms,
fish libraries, alt-lakes,

and the last
oyster I sipped
from its little
rocky basin—
did it have just
the weak-with-Arctic

-icemelt, hydrocarbon
tang of this
particular
bad year of ocean?
Maybe a relic?

I could ask my Brooklynites
who ride the elevated F
to look up from their phones,
but it's hard
to tell the harbor's distant blue
through those tiny, glaring windows
from simulation—could they be sure

it was real, it was now?

I've searched
the papers, but the things
these days that pass unsaid
are world-size. I might be
the last to know
what Matthew Arnold long ago
discerned,
the *melancholy, long, withdrawing roar*
of the Sea of Faith *retreating*
down the vast edges drear
and naked shingles of the world—
maybe withdrawn
into a subduction zone?

Could you swear, have you checked?
I mean, within the hour?

As easily as you wake,
your round eyes dry,
and blink,
it could be gone,
since even its superstorms

and rogue waves, seen
in proportion, are a slick
on an eight-thousand-mile
sphere of rock,
a ball rolled through wet grass
into hot sun.
                    Once I was surer
what was what—the word
under my feet, the sky, the stars,
and from the shore,
Relax, my mother called,
lie back and put your arms out straight
and it will hold you.

(addresses in the manner of issa)

Lilacs!
How long
did I sleep?

If you stay
way up there, spider,
we're OK.

Sunlight
lighter, noticing
that I notice.

Three days
of rain—it's restless,
our little stream.

First warm night—
there's such a thing
as mosquitoes!

If there were two of you,
Moon, would you have stopped
to have this little talk?

Magenta, powder blue—
Dawn, I wouldn't
wear those!

First day warm enough
for butterflies—no one's
walking straight.

Never mind, robin,
I don't have a real job
either.

Noon—the sun
small and hot
from its climb.

Hairs stirring
on my wrist—the air's
little legs.

This many hours
past dawn, more talkers
than singers.

End of summer, sills
brimming with wings
        breath makes fly again.

What was wrong,
monarch,
    with being a caterpillar?

                        Chewing in the wall
                stops,
                    hearing its name.

(So dark!
Now where did I
put that moon?)

Not a Bird

No more birds,
please, too easily
exceeding us—

their automatic song,
their just-out-of-reach
supernal softness, and of course

the whole Flight Thing.
Envious? Yes,
but we've never really liked

the people most like them—
kissless, jittering,
as if touch were voltage. No,

birds make us feel bad—
let's sing, instead,
this beetle, who has rayed

directly through glass
to be a bad miracle
in the family room. *Beetle*

has the same root as
bite, which mostly, it is said,
they don't, though I have never

not swished one off my hand
too fast to find out
firsthand. As for this one,

I can hardly forbear
whacking it or sliding
under it

a sheet of paper
as it crosses what must seem
(waterless, harsh, beige)

a brutal, days-wide
Sahara of carpet. So painfully
deliberate, even though aimless,

is its crawling
that it feels like counting,
the one two… six

distinct limps, the legs
not quite part of the thing they carry,
like pallbearers, yet when a beetle

suddenly remembers it can fly—
loud, blundering, underpowered—
you see why it usually walks.

Such labor! As if just getting
from one place to another
were a somewhat mechanical compromise

with more complex yearnings,
as indeed it always is.
Just look at their life cycle—

egg to larva to pupa to adult,
which seems like a lot of magic tricks
no one *oohs* at, just

to arrive at beetle. If only
I had kept track of friends
from high school, better to know

what becomes what. Though with us—
right?—it's less metamorphosis
than reorganization, like the earth's,

our difficult ranges
smoothed down or sucked under,
what once seemed deep and hot

thrust up to cool
and solidify—
the same old stuff, that is,

in a configuration a little easier
to live with. Like us,
beetles, of whatever size,

seem a little bulkier
than ideal—is it too sad
to say they lighten, by comparison,

my obsession with lightness?
Anyway temporarily,
since gazing at myself

even this long in their dark
mirror, I feel old heaviness
returning, a song

letting me down
exactly where I was,
only more so,

as if I were one of night's black leaves
brought indoors
that had somehow kept its night-black glow.

Bird
dropping the white
of the sky.

Pines

Pine—the tree, that is—grows from a root
that means *to swell,* from which we also get
the word *fat,* and by extension
Eire and the *Pierian* springs, for their fertility.
But the pine in *to pine for* or *to pine away*
stems from a root *to pay for* or *atone*
which gives us *penalty* and *punish* and *pain.*
Somehow two thoughts, on different sides
of a shearing fault of language, have slid together
and stuck, for our lifetimes, anyway, at the sound *pine.*

It's not so common, in this practical century,
for lovers to pine away, and as our climate warms,
pines are retreating higher, but late as it is,
anyone sleepless will hear the sound of the wind
thinning through pines as pained. Maybe at first
they were a little strange with each other,
but it's natural, now, that *pine* and *pine* are *pine.*
Just as, when two who met on a trail one morning
are still talking at sunset, something other
than matching their strides is keeping them together.

Coming in late
from the garden,
    dark on my hands.

Ode to the World as a Cat

They say, alone as we are, and overruled, and sick with dreams,
we need a companion to settle our hearts, an animal maybe,
and World, you are with me, though always turning away
with a cool, feline disregard, horizon after horizon,
as if it's beneath or beyond you to answer my questions
(oh, they are not even questions—hurts, wonders)
except with your distant rumblings, lying out in the sun,
and the quick-changing weathers of your eyes
that surely don't mean what I hope or fear they mean.

Often we do not need each other all day.
You are losing yourself in one vista after another,
and I am lost in memories, loves, resentments, nothing to you.
If sometimes you flash or brush against me, it's an accident,
just your thinking of nothing in particular as you wake,
stretching to full length and turning over in the sun.
How fitting that you love only the unreadable sun,
which sees nothing, which cares nothing for you.

And then all night—you are happy to be left out all night—
you do what you do. I hear the cries, animal or wind or human,
but in the morning, you are at the door, sunny and uncomplicated.
Like a cat, you taste no sweetness, not even your own.
Like a cat, you are red-green color-blind, like a cat,
you cannot see your ripe fruits lying in the grass,
you cannot tell the blood of the ripped prey
I find in the morning garden from the flow of its leaves.

Life or death, it doesn't matter, you seem to say,
which saddens me, too human after all,
I with groundless regrets and resolutions, groundless desires,
alone and overruled and sick with dreams,
though maybe it's what I need most, your indifference.

You can't tell if I'm ugly or fat or disheveled,
stupid or smart is the same to you, good or bad at love,
even old doesn't matter, old as you are, and what do you care
if I say that our springs, growing fainter, are warmer,
if I linger in winter sunsets, surprised at my own surprise,
now that it seems too late to be anything but free,
out here, alone together, each the last of our kind?

Wanderer's Night Song (II)

Over the hills,
stillness.
In miles of leaves
you sense
hardly a breath.
The birds have quieted in the forest.
Wait a little,
you as well
will come to rest.

Goethe

5   After the Seasons

Autumn is all the seasons in palimpsest.

Malcolm de Chazal

Even our winter,
over. Now the fifth season—
all of them at once.

Autumn Evening

Lord, all this cool day so late in the year
that curious creature of yours—me—
like a squirrel piecing a nest together,
has been shifting fallen leaves and branches
from where it seemed they shouldn't be
to where it seems they should,
then making, by rules too old to remember,
a dinner of savors and herbs to suit the season,
and sitting awhile to think what my daughters
might be up to, one tending window plants,
the other, maybe, on her phone
distractedly driving (I wish she wouldn't).

I send them to do whatever they must do,
wishing them wordlessly good night,
since now it is very late, Lord,
and I should let what I love be what it is
and attend to what is only mine,
letting my feet gratefully unshoe each other,
shutting the books on their markers,
and putting the notes to self and keys and glasses
exactly in place, since who can tell
what summons might come in the night
so that I might need to find them in the dark.

(way) after bashō

Crows
settling among crows—
autumn evening.

No rain—
you see what the reservoir's
been thinking.

Raking leaves
till they're invisible—
autumn evening.

The way
their lights are on
no one's home.

Beautiful
the fallen leaves, but deer
won't touch them.

Tears, idle tears—
what did it used to be,
this smoke?

At the foot
of the last scarecrow—
agnostic crows.

Winter sunset—
I put down groceries
to unlock the door.

Leaves now and then
blowing down the road
autumn left on.

No roof yet—
first snow
  chilling the bedrooms.

  Steeped
in a trillion nights, the moon
  undarkened.

January days
a half hour longer—
  this half hour.

Sparrows
bathing in a footprint
of sky.

Spring everywhere—
a couple of trees
    remember they are dead.

Centuries back,
sign says, there was a battle.
Did I win?

Splash
in the old pond—taste
of blood on my lip.

White butterflies
spiraling up a column
that isn't there.

Across the path—
tree that fell last night
still falling.

I'm just a visitor,
Spring.
   Autumn evening.

Vectors 5.2

PG-50: Aphorisms and Ten-Second Essays

It's soothing when the newly dead are way older than I am. This guy was ninety-five. His picture—middle-aged, with archaic glasses—freezes him in the 1970s. But even when they are my age and live in my town and share so many of my habits and interests that it's upsetting, I keep on. Since never in recorded history has anyone died while reading the obituaries.

*

When we're talking happily, life is long enough. It's when I'm sitting around restless and bored with it that I lament how little is left.

*

The years get shorter but the hours are just as long.

*

It's not so much that I'm hard of hearing, just that it takes me longer to get back from wherever I go in my head these days. Sometimes I don't make sense of your words till a second or two after I've said *What?* Or an hour after, or a year.

*

Getting older is like downsizing. Life is suddenly crowded with stuff I used to store in the future.

*

All the time I saved—where has that bank gone now that I want to make a withdrawal?

*

The play called *Life* is about having all the time in the world. So it's the old who have to be great actors. The young are just those lovable kinds of stars who play only themselves.

*

Phrase never heard: *That talented old man!*

*

Resolution: I will no longer think, hearing the apocalyptic News, *No worries, I'll be dead before the worst happens.*

*

I like hanging out with kids, since Youth is contagious. Only now, like my colds—like the years—it's shorter and less intense.

*

I'm far more likely to say *I'm too old for that* than *That's too young for me,* maybe hoping someone will tell me I'm not.

*

Old friends are best because they relieve me of the foolish hope that I might possibly have become someone that they don't know all about.

*

Seems like the older I get, the fewer reasons there are for doing the things I don't want to, which makes them both harder and easier.

*

No pain, no gain? No pain, no *pain*.

*

Over and over, what I thought was the work was a distraction, what I thought was a distraction turned out to be the real work.

*

When someone asks if I've read a particular book, and it's been decades, I should probably just say *No* and let them talk. It would make just as much sense, actually, to disown large swaths of the past. Things I did, people I knew way back, even who I was, aren't necessarily realer now than things I've only read about.

*

All that reading and talking, and still I don't know if all of us are really different or really the same.

*

So many days I forget everything except what's here and now. I'm a floating island, shaped by a past that's no longer beneath me. Though every once in a while a toy I haven't seen in years, the odor from a long-unopened drawer, or a photo of a dead friend seem to remember *me*.

*

Twenty-five thousand days, and not one of them do I know by heart.

*

I thought memory was an endless surveillance tape, but it's note cards thrown in a drawer.

*

The great mysteries seem tip-of-the-tongue, as if once I understood them for an instant and am trying to remember, the shadows of birds that passed the window before I could look up.

*

What keeps me from knowing is thinking I already know.

*

We want the little mysteries to be solved, the big ones to persist.

*

The other day I thought I'd erased all my files. It felt great, like instantly losing twenty pounds.

*

Learning is hard and slow, though not as slow and hard as unlearning.

*

Experience teaches that experience won't entirely suffice. The god who made the world is not necessarily the one to make it better.

*

First I worked hard to be modern, then I worked harder not to be.

*

The urban legend that the living outnumber the dead suggests how much help we need to escape the past. It's not enough that our moment is different from all others just by being Now. We want a majority vote.

*

The only things we don't get over are those we never realized we had to get over.

*

SF premise: I upload my mind into a computer and they download it into a clone of me when I die. Would that still be me? I'm guessing the majority answer in the sophomore philosophy seminar is *No way. When the lights go out, it's me who dies; I don't cross to that other life.* I can't disagree, but the other answer—that if no one can tell the difference, there is no difference— appeals to me more and more now that my job in the world, whatever it was, seems closer to over. I'm not as confident as the sophomores that there's something inside me uniquely unknown and unexpressed. More and more, I'm only what matters to those I would leave behind. If that clone could be for them whatever I was, dying might still be painful and terrifying, but death itself would look like a smaller matter.

*

Just think of him—all those memories that seem to be his, yet no idea, really, how he got there. Oh.

*

The eyes of one god close. The eyes of another god open. And there was already light.

*

We're moved by the thought that some of the stars we see are already dead, though the news hasn't reached us yet. But the stars visible to the naked eye are pretty close—their light might be four years old, or maybe one thousand. What are the chances any of them have died in that interval, a blink in their ten-billion-year lifespan? It's more likely that you yourself will die in the minutes you're looking up at them, or down at these.

*

It's like they say—the great miracle, over and over, is that we're here. Though how could it be any other way?—since if we weren't, we wouldn't know.

*

When my father died, I found one in the basement, one in his bureau: two canisters of ashes, no names, no dates. I buried them in our backyard, probably illegally, at a respectable distance from each other, since if they were who I suspected, they probably wouldn't have wanted to be all that close together for eternity. Ten years later, I'm not sure exactly where they are. At first I felt bad for forgetting, but now I think what happened was that they slept off all their attachments and flowed underground out of our memories.

*

When you're the last one who remembers, it's finally OK to forget.

*

A half hour into the woods, two tires, still on their rims, leaning against a tree. It's impossible to imagine anyone rolling them in this far, or ever rolling them out again. Maybe they were already there when the tree sprouted, lifting them, and will be there forever because time does not know how to change them.

*

I keep imagining a work composed entirely of endings.

*

I'll be so embarrassed, Death. Years of gossiping about you, though we've never met.

*

My epitaph: *Against his will, he mostly did what he wanted.*

*

Old December's bareness every where. Except right there: a single branch, fully leafed but all brown. I've been tempted to admire what seems like bleak persistence. But if you look closely, there's a white break where it was snapped downward in a storm, so that the tree's signal *Summer is ending* couldn't get through. Once you notice one, you start seeing them everywhere, the ones who never got the message, *Blaze, let go.*

*

Out at the edge of feeling these days, a wisp of *Safe now; I'll die before they find out!* Find out what?

So late, my lamp
flickers—struggling to stay lit
or go out?

In my hands
the *Times*
    turning to yesterday's.

Small hours
colder—rain
    starting to tick.

Epilogue in Stone

Some your tires
spit sideways,

some you lever
out of the garden,
size of a head, weight of a man,

others only
glaciers will move again.

*

Lower one into the old pond
slowly enough, unbearably slowly,
and it will float,

and a pebble thrown into fog
may never land,

and the moon falls
one kilometer per second
slowly, slowly, slowly enough

that it could rest on your hand.

*

The one your kick uprooted,
wrong side up,
burns in terrible air.

Others are exoplanets
visible only
as the wobble or occultation of a star.

All stones are broken stones
I was going to say.

*

There was a first stone, surely,
before they were everywhere,

their long weathering suffusing
even the air,

so hard by now that, stair by stair,
a plane can climb it,

and dawn is the damp cool
under a stone,

and a little dust of stone is evening,
and the cold headwind is stone.

*

When you have lain a billion years
under stars,
it is less clear, the difference
between stone and star.

Hard to know if the stones
have fallen as far as they will fall

or will rise,
yet still, like them,

I dream of weighing on my love
nothing.

*

Klee painted them
as flowers
teetering on stems.
It is true they are harder
and harder to lift, yet it feels
truer and truer
that they might wonderfully,
fearfully
drift away.

*

When young, I thought their self-sufficiency
would suffice.

I grew up modern, I had been taught
not to say *tears*.

But Du Fu says, and truly,
that an old man cries easily,

glass so full a grain of sand
overbrims it.

I will not say *tears*. I will say that in my eyes
there is stone so hot and thin it flows.

*

They too in spring winds strain
to fly, to stay.

When yellow leaves, or none, or few do hang...

If life is a year, then this is
November, just about the day
I'm thinking it'll never get cold
and it gets cold; if life is a day,
then now is the darkening, serious
but not quite deep enough to sleep in;
if life is an hour, then I'm near the end
of a story I might or might not
finish in an hour. But life is a minute,
and suddenly looking up
from the page, who can tell
whether it's the middle or end
or beginning of a minute?

After the Flood

Surely it had been forty *years*
since we turned away, forsaking all others,
to do what it seemed we had to do,
hearing the rain set in that would rain so long,
but when we walked out that first morning after,
the roads steamed, and, here and there,
there were leaves already dry to the touch,
as if it had been… what, forty minutes?

And minute by minute our children's laughter
receded into the woods, too late to call back,
and the land widened as we listened—mowers, traffic.
It was somehow full already, this new world
that we seemed to remember, that we were called to love,
though it was not for us, because it was not for us,
for better or for worse, for richer or poorer,
and with this ring, set with a drop of rain.

Notes

"Incredulous Essay on Hummingbirds." In normal sleep, birds *do* dream—it seems from patterns of brain activation that they may dream, among other things, of singing. I don't know whether the "torpor" of hummingbirds is deep enough to shut those dreams down, but I hold a valid Poetic License from the State of New Jersey.

"Otherwise: Aphorisms and Ten-Second Essays" and "PG-50: Aphorisms and Ten-Second Essays." The "Vectors 5.1" and "Vectors 5.2" are just bookkeeping for a project that began with *Vectors: Aphorisms and Ten-Second Essays* in 2001 and has now spread into a fifth book.

Not sure I'm calling these three-line microlyrics *haiku*. But they are certainly homage to what I can understand of Bashō and Issa. Or rather, what I can understand of R.H. Blyth's *Haiku* and Robert Hass's *Essential Haiku,* which are always on my desk.

"Now." The Planck time is the time it takes light to travel the Planck length, which is 1.6×10^{-35} meters, somewhat shorter than an aphorism. In theory, it's a quantum of time—there can be no shorter interval. "Sleep-wake cycle": light sleepers will recognize a tendency to see the clock at ninety-minute intervals. This cycle of alertness persists through the daylight hours.

"Not an Artichoke." "Neruda": in "Oda a la alcachofa."

"With a Grain of Salt." Mark Kurlansky's *Salt: A World History* is the source of several facts used in this poem: e.g., in the lines about the seventeenth-century diarist John Evelyn.

"Essay Slightly in Advance of the Discovery of Element 120." Last time I checked, there were 118 elements on the Periodic Table. Only 94 of them occur naturally on Earth—tiny and very fleeting quantities of the others are created in atom-smashers.

"On the Fly." Maggots, wounds, and surgeons: true. Though the maggots used to clean wounds are raised in sterile conditions.

"Wanderer's Night Song (II)." I fell in love with Goethe's untranslatable whisper of a poem, a sequel to "Wandrers Nachtlied," in my first week of college and finally got around to translating it:

Ein Gleiches

Über allen Gipfeln
Ist Ruh,
In allen Wipfeln
Spürest du
Kaum einen Hauch;
Die Vögelein schweigen im Walde.
Warte nur, balde
Ruhest du auch

"Autumn is all the seasons in palimpsest." Malcolm de Chazal, *Sens-Plastique* [*Plastic Sense*], translated by Irving Weiss. "L'automne, c'est toutes les saisons en palimpseste."

"(way) after bashō." "Tears, idle tears" is perhaps the best known of the songs in Tennyson's *The Princess*. "So sad, so strange, the days that are no more."

"PG-50: Aphorisms and Ten-Second Essays." "Old December's bareness every where": Shakespeare, sonnet 97.

"When yellow leaves, or none, or few do hang..." I'm in treatment for compulsive quotation of Shakespeare's sonnet 73.

About the Author

James Richardson's collections of poems, aphorisms, and microforms include *During* (2016), the National Book Award finalist *By the Numbers* (2010), the National Book Critics Circle Award finalist *Interglacial* (2004), and *Vectors: Aphorisms and Ten-Second Essays* (2001). He teaches at Princeton University and lives in New Jersey with his wife, the scholar and critic Constance W. Hassett. They have two daughters.

Poetry is vital to language and living. Since 1972, Copper Canyon Press has published extraordinary poetry from around the world to engage the imaginations and intellects of readers, writers, booksellers, librarians, teachers, students, and donors.

WE ARE GRATEFUL FOR THE MAJOR SUPPORT PROVIDED BY:

THE PAUL G. ALLEN
FAMILY FOUNDATION

Lannan

TO LEARN MORE ABOUT UNDERWRITING COPPER CANYON PRESS TITLES, PLEASE CALL 360-385-4925 EXT. 103

WE ARE GRATEFUL FOR THE MAJOR SUPPORT PROVIDED BY:

Anonymous

Jill Baker and Jeffrey Bishop

Anne and Geoffrey Barker

Donna and Matthew Bellew

John Branch

Diana Broze

John R. Cahill

The Beatrice R. and Joseph A. Coleman Foundation

The Currie Family Fund

Laurie and Oskar Eustis

Mimi Gardner Gates

Gull Industries Inc. on behalf of William True

The Trust of Warren A. Gummow

Carolyn and Robert Hedin

Phil Kovacevich and Eric Wechsler

Lakeside Industries Inc. on behalf of Jeanne Marie Lee

Maureen Lee and Mark Busto

Ellie Mathews and Carl Youngmann as The North Press

Petunia Charitable Fund and adviser Elizabeth Hebert

John W. Phillips

Gay Phinny

Suzie Rapp and Mark Hamilton

Adam and Lynn Rauch

Emily and Dan Raymond

Jill and Bill Ruckelshaus

Cynthia Sears

Kim and Jeff Seely

Daniel M. Waggoner

Barbara and Charles Wright

Caleb Young as C. Young Creative

The dedicated interns and faithful volunteers of Copper Canyon Press

The Chinese character for poetry is made up of two parts:
"word" and "temple." It also serves as pressmark for
Copper Canyon Press.

The poems are set in Adobe Garamond.
Book design and composition by Phil Kovacevich.